ॐ



# Mandukya

# UPANISHAD

## Essence and Sanskrit Grammar

**Ashwini** was born in Ludhiana in his mother's home and completed his pre-University from Govt. College for Boys. He has also written texts on Sanskrit Grammar delving into Panini's Ashtadhyayi.

**From the same Author:**

Bhagavad Gita for Chanting
Bhagavad Gita Applied Wisdom

Tao Te Ching Brahman
Ishavasya Upanishad: Essence and Sanskrit Grammar
Katha Upanishad: Essence and Sanskrit Grammar
Narada Bhakti Sutra: Essence and Sanskrit Grammar
Bhagavad Gita Dhyana Yoga: Commentary and Grammar
Patanjali Yoga Sutras: Essence and Sanskrit Grammar

The Sanskrit Alphabet
Ashtadhyayi of Panini Complete
Dhatupatha Sutras Enumerated
Dhatupatha Verbs in 5 Lakaras
Dhatupatha of Panini: Accented Roots with English Meanings and Verbs iii/1 forms in Present Tense

Rudra Puja: Simple Complete Profound
Rudra Puja Mantras

ॐ

# Mandukya

# UPANISHAD

## Essence and Sanskrit Grammar

Ashwini Kumar Aggarwal

जय गुरुदेव

ISBN10: 1-0991-9354-0
ISBN13: 978-1-0991-9354-5
Paperback Edition



Title: **Mandukya Upanishad**
SubTitle: **Essence and Sanskrit Grammar**

Printed and Published by Ashwini Kumar Aggarwal
The Art of Living Centre
147 Punjabi Bagh, Patiala 147001
Punjab, India

https://advaita56.weebly.com/
Devotees of Sri Sri Ravi Shankar Ashram

https://www.artofliving.org/

18th March 2019, Lord's Bathinda Punjab Darshan
Somvar Pradosh, Dvadashi, Shukla Paksha, Uttarayana
Vikram Samvat 2075 Virodhakrit, Saka Era 1940 Vilambi

1st Edition March 2019

जय गुरुदेव

# Dedication

Sri Sri Ravi Shankar

who gave us **OM namah shivaya** slow chant

# Acknowledgements

Lord's historic Bathinda, Punjab visit after a successful Vigyan Bhairav in Chandigarh-Panchkula and interaction with CEOs in Ludhiana. Then on chopper to Moga and finally Mandi Gobindgarh.

## Blessing

All the Saints in the past, when they went deep into meditation, they just heard Om. So, Om means many things. It means love, eternity, purity, peace. Om is made up of several dhatus: 'Ah' 'Oo' 'Ma'. Just ‘Ah’ has 19 meanings.

The total prana is represented by one syllable OM. Before birth, we were part of that sound and after death we will merge with that sound; the SOUND of the Spirit.

Sri Sri Ravi Shankar
Birthday Celebrations, Montreal
Q & A in Canadian Ashram, May 10, 2012

## Preface

Upanishads are verses from the Vedas that have been compiled as independent and complete sets. Those verses in the Vedas that amplify the greatness of man, his soul's journey, and his ultimate purpose are termed as Upanishads.

Traditionally the verses in each Veda have been classified as Mantra portion or Brahmana portion. **Mantra verses are action oriented. Brahmana verses are thinking oriented.**

Within the Brahmana portion, a further sub-classification of verses has been done, namely Brahmana-Aranyaka-Upanishad. Technically Brahmana means planning, discussion and analysis. Aranyaka means research and philosophy. Upanishad means essential thought or teaching or guiding principle.

Upanishad verses are those that are found at the end. Thus aptly named **Vedanta**. Literal meaning ending-portion of the Veda. Spiritual connotation core-design-crux-essence.

| Veda | |
| --- | --- |
| Mantra Verses (Samhita) | Brahmana Verses |
| | Brahmana<br>Aranyaka<br>Upanishad |

Adi Shankaracharya's masterly commentary on eleven Upanishads is the de-facto standard for Vedanta. These eleven have been named the principal Upanishads. Though it is said there are 1180 Upanishads written over a period of a thousand years, more than a couple of thousand years ago, actual manuscripts available are around 108 only.

A chart that lists the eleven Upanishads commented on in detail by Sankara.

| Rigveda | Samaveda | <u>Shukla Yajurveda</u><br>Krishna Yajurveda | Atharvaveda |
|---|---|---|---|
| Gives the fundamental laws of creation | Gives the intrinsic harmony within creation | Gives the specific design, administrative and governing principles for a family or a nation | Gives the specific ritucharya and dinacharya for an individual |
| **Aitareya** | Kena<br>**Chandogya** | Ishavasya<br>**<u>Brihadaranyaka</u>**<br>KATHA<br>Taittiriya<br>Shvetashvatara | Prashna<br>**Mandukya**<br>Mundaka |
| प्रज्ञानम् ब्रह्म | तत् त्वम् असि | अहं ब्रह्म अस्मि | अयम् आत्मा ब्रह्म |

Four great illuminating statements or mahavakyas are listed above with their corresponding Upanishads in **bold**.

Remember that Vedic Sanskrit text cannot be literally translated into English. Such literal meanings are rather skimpy, irrelevant or fall flat.

A thought that emerges from the deep silent mind has to be sculpted with stoic precision. One has to dive into the great literature and come up with nuggets that crystallize the essence of a bygone era that knew no deprivation.

Mandukya Upanishad is from the Atharva Veda. It elucidates the four topics; Waking state, Dreaming State, Deep Sleep state, and the ever present yet seldom known Transcendental state.

## Contents

## Etymology of Upanishad

व्युत्पत्ति

Consider Adi Shankaracharya's derivation of the word 'Upanishad' as given in his bhashyam on the Katha Upanishad.

उप + नि + षद् + क्विप् –> उपनिषद्

The Sanskrit root from Dhatupatha 1c - 854, 6c - 1427

षद्लृ विशरण–गति–अवसादनेषु has the three meanings,

namely विशरण = wither, गति = attain, अवसादनं = sit.

In the context of wisdom, we can say

- wither away one's stupidity
- attain liberation
- sit with a conviction

The upasarga उप stands for nearness, closeness.

The upasarga नि stands for delving into, intense.

The pratyaya क्विप् makes a noun, and while joining, it vanishes entirely.

Thus the word 'Upanishad' is formed, and it has the meaning of destroying one's ignorance and gaining freedom, when we sit devotedly at the feet of the Master.

# Prayer - Shanti Mantra

ॐ

भद्रं कर्णेभिः शृणुयाम देवाः । भद्रं पश्ये माक्षभिर् यजत्राः ।

स्थिरैरङ्गैस् तुष्टुवाꣳसस्तनूभिः । व्यशेम देवहितं यदायुः ॥

स्वस्ति न इन्द्रो वृद्धश्रवाः । स्वस्ति नः पूषा विश्ववेदाः ।

स्वस्ति नस्तार्क्ष्यो अरिष्टनेमिः । स्वस्ति नो बृहस्पतिर्दधातु ॥

ॐ शान्तिः शान्तिः शान्तिः ॥

**Shanti Mantra**

O Divine Wisdom!
May our ears listen to the sacred and the auspicious.
May our eyes see the propitious as we come together to partake of wisdom.
May our limbs be firm and body attuned to long endurances.
May our senses function with full alertness and
May the sense of contentment be strong.
May our good thoughts form a discus to shield us and
May our education give us a shining personality.

Peace in our heart, in our body and in our environs.

## Verse 1 OM is ALL

---

Adverbs in Sanskrit are indeclinable generally.

In this verse, the word अन्यत् can be used in the sense of an adverb and also in the sense of an adjective!

अक्षरम् = It is a common practice in Sanskrit grammar to use a "hyphen" to indicate compounds.

Compound or समास is frequently encountered in Sanskrit literature. It has a beauty and a brevity.

*(Most teachers will give the case of* अक्षरम् *and* सर्वं *as nominative but we prefer accusative for clarity.)*

ओमित्येतदक्षरमिदं सर्वं तस्योपव्याख्यानं भूतं भवद्भविष्यदिति सर्वमोङ्कार एव । यच्चान्यत्त्रिकालातीतं तदप्योङ्कार एव ॥ १

omityetadakṣaramidaṃ sarvaṃ tasyopavyākhyānaṃ bhūtaṃ bhavadbhaviṣyaditi sarvamoṅkāra eva |
yaccānyattrikālātītaṃ tadapyoṅkāra eva || 1

प०)

ओम् इति एतत् अ–क्षरम् इदं सर्वं तस्य उप-व्याख्यानं भूतं भवत् भविष्यत् इति सर्वम् ओङ्कारः एव । यत् च अन्यत् त्रिकाल–अतीतं तत् अपि ओङ्कारः एव ॥

अ०)

ॐ [0] इति[0] एतत् [n1/1] अक्षरम् [n2/1] इदं [n2/1] सर्वं [n2/1];

Om. Full stop. This imperishable it all (is);

तस्य [n6/1] उपव्याख्यानं [n1/1], भूतं [PPP क्त n1/1] भवत् [PrPA शतृ n1/1] भविष्यत् [FPA शतृ n1/1] इति [0] सर्वम् [n1/1] ॐकारः [m1/1] एव [0] ।

यत् [n1/1] च [0] अन्यत् [0] त्रिकालातीतं [n1/1], तत् [n1/1] अपि [0] ॐकारः [m1/1] एव [0] ॥

इति = Full stop. तस्य = of it. उपव्याख्यानं = relative description. भूतं भवत् भविष्यत् = the Past Present Future. इति सर्वम् ॐकारः एव =this all Om Sound alone (is). अन्यत् [0] = Moreover (adverb). / अन्यत् [n1/1] Other than (adjective). त्रिकालातीतं = beyond the concept of time. That which does not belong to a time domain.

1 This world is a light and sound show. All of it here is just name and form. Each movie, app or game is two dimensional - audio and video.

Light can easily be shut by dropping the eyelids or covered by an eye-scarf. It is sound that has a bigger dimension that can't be just warded off.

Close your eyes and listen. Be still and let the waves speak. Become aware of the breeze whispering. Hark and hear the heartbeat, know it is a pulse.

This creation pulsates day and night. As the stars twinkle the biggest heroes get known by their one-liners and administrators by their quotable quotes.

Know this is all Om. Know it all as Aum. When a baby is born Om is heard and when bells peal they chorus Aum. Ever since the bow of Space strung the arrow of Time, Om reverberated.

Om is manifest yet unmanifest too. Aum is the seed and the sprout and also the space and the sunshine.

Aum has been chanted in homes and workplaces. Om is the octave and Aum is the harmonic. Om is and will be.

*(Most teachers will give the case of* ब्रह्म *and* चतुष्पात् *as nominative but we prefer accusative.)*

## Verse 2 Mahavakya अयम् आत्मा ब्रह्म

सर्वं ह्येतद् ब्रह्मायमात्मा ब्रह्म सोऽयमात्मा चतुष्पात् ॥ २
sarvaṃ hyetad brahmāyamātmā brahma so'yamātmā catuṣpāt || 2

प०) सर्वं हि एतत् ब्रह्म अयम् आत्मा ब्रह्म सः अयम् आत्मा चतुष्पात् ॥

अ०) सर्वं $^{n1/1}$ हि $^{0}$ एतत् $^{n2/1}$ ब्रह्म $^{n2/1}$ ।
All verily this Brahman (is).
अयम् $^{m1/1}$ आत्मा $^{m1/1}$ ब्रह्म $^{n2/1}$ । This Soul Brahman (is).
सः $^{m1/1}$, अयम् $^{m1/1}$ आत्मा $^{m1/1}$, चतुष्पात् $^{n2/1}$ ॥ (all) That, (and) This Soul, four states (has).

चतुष्पात् from stem चतुष्पद् $^{n}$ ।

ब्रह्म from stem ब्रह्मन् $^{n}$ । Note. We have a masculine stem ब्रह्मन् $^{m}$, that declines as ब्रह्मा in the nominative. It has a different meaning as well. ब्रह्मन् $^{n}$ is the invisible source of everything, whereas ब्रह्मन् $^{m}$ is a visible manifestation and a particular facet of ब्रह्मन् $^{n}$ ।

अयम् आत्मा ब्रह्म । Termed in Vedantic lore as a Mahavakya, a statement that is most powerful in the meditative techniques. A statement that unlocks the secret of creation. A statement that leads one to transcendence. That has the force to overcome misery.

2 Know it by another name too. Brahman. The Eternity. Soul. The Center. with 4 spokes. rests on 4 pillars. has 4 expressions. 4 modes of transaction.

Close your eyes and know you are the Father and the Flame, also the Son and the Stranger.

You are known at Home and in the Workplace. You are also known in the Game and in the Temple.

# Verse 3 Awake the Emperor

जागरितस्थानो बहिष्प्रज्ञः सप्ताङ्ग एकोनविंशतिमुखः स्थूलभुग्वैश्वानरः प्रथमः पादः ॥ ३

jāgaritasthāno bahiṣprajñaḥ saptāṅga ekonaviṃśatimukhaḥ sthūlabhugvaiśvānaraḥ prathamaḥ pādaḥ ll 3

प०) जागरित–स्थानः बहिष्–प्रज्ञः सप्ताङ्गः एकोन–विंशति–मुखः स्थूल–भुक् वैश्वानरः प्रथमः पादः ॥

अ०) जागरितस्थानः m1/1 बहिष्प्रज्ञः m1/1 सप्ताङ्गः m1/1 एकोनविंशतिमुखः m1/1 स्थूलभुक् m1/1 वैश्वानरः m1/1 प्रथमः m1/1 पादः m1/1 ॥

जागरितस्थानः = the one in waking state. बहिष्प्रज्ञः = the one with outward senses and attention. सप्ताङ्गः = the seven limbed. एकोनविंशतिमुखः = the one with nineteen attributes. स्थूलभुक् = enjoyer of the gross physical stuff. वैश्वानरः = world emperor. प्रथमः = first. पादः = phase.

स्थानः from stem स्थानिन् m ।

वैश्वानरः = Taddhita from विश्व–नरः ।

3 Your first expression is Wakefulness. All senses streaming. Memory and Intellect in strong positioning.

While awake you may not be alert. You may be tired and dull. You may be in stupor, panic, hallucination or wonder! There is a chance you are day dreaming without your knowledge!

Aims and Ambitions govern the *waker*. Me and Mine mark his boundaries.

The waking state is a reflection. It is bound by the intelligence, the education, the resources and the responsibility. It is bound by the body and its limits in the space time continuum. It is bound by the mind and how far it can soar.

Vaishvanara or state of processing all inputs. In computer language - Booted up state.

**19 = 10+9 = 20-1. (1+9 = 10, 1+0 = 1 = Brahman = Turiya or transcendental state).** One is the first number and Nine the last in a decimal set, and Nineteen is the 8$^{th}$ prime number. Our meditations are mostly 19-20 minutes. Potassium also known as Kalium, that is indispensable for living cells, has the atomic number 19. 19 can be written symbolically in various ways, e.g.1,6+3 (163 figures in Ramanujan constant). 1,1+8. (118 eighteen means victory in Sanskrit). The Metonic cycle is 19 years.

## Verse 4 Dream the Spark

स्वप्नस्थानोऽन्तःप्रज्ञः सप्ताङ्ग एकोनविंशतिमुखः प्रविविक्तभुक्तैजसो द्वितीयः पादः ॥ ४

svapnasthāno'ntaḥprajñaḥ saptāṅga ekonaviṃśatimukhaḥ praviviktabhuktaijaso dvitīyaḥ pādaḥ ॥ 4

प०) स्वप्न–स्थानः अन्तःप्रज्ञः सप्ताङ्गः एकोन–विंशति–मुखः प्रविविक्त–भुक् तैजसः द्वितीयः पादः ॥

अ०) स्वप्नस्थानः $^{m1/1}$ अन्तःप्रज्ञः $^{m1/1}$ सप्ताङ्गः $^{m1/1}$ एकोनविंशतिमुखः $^{m1/1}$ प्रविविक्तभुक् $^{m1/1}$ तैजसः $^{m1/1}$ द्वितीयः $^{m1/1}$ पादः $^{m1/1}$ ॥

स्वप्नस्थानः = the one in dream state अन्तःप्रज्ञः = the one with senses shut. सप्ताङ्गः = the seven limbed one.

एकोनविंशतिमुखः = the one-less-than-twenty faceted.

प्रविविक्तभुक् = enjoyer of the unmanifest subtle realm.

तैजसः = the one with spark, i.e. looks inert but is actually alive. द्वितीयः = second पादः = phase.

तैजसः = a Taddhita derivative from तेजसः to mean the one with vigor. (even though in the dream state he appears inert).

4 Your second state is Dream. It is usually without sense input. More or less without memory and intellect functioning.

And how is that? In a sleeping dream most of us can be said to have switched off the senses, memory and intellect.

But for sure a few have these faculties on while dreaming. Latent desires sprout and take center stage. Cravings and Aversions rule the night.

What about the day dream? What about the fantasy and the building castles in the air? What about when you are imagining - as in a creative thought, or in illusion or even in a drugged state?

What about the Yogis or the ever wakeful?

The dream state surpasses the waking state. It has fewer limitations of body and mind. Where one might go in the dream can be another galaxy or somewhere in the Satya Yuga or far into the future.

This state is known to be the cause of numerous inventions! And why should it be superior to the waking? Simply because it is more easily forgotten and the slate is cleaner and dream impressions are more fluid than waking imprints.
Tejas or the state of being powerfully inactive. Standby.

# Verse 5 Deep Sleep the Bliss

यत्र सुप्तो न कञ्चन कामं कामयते न कञ्चन स्वप्नं पश्यति तत्सुषुप्तम् ।

सुषुप्तस्थान एकीभूतः प्रज्ञानघन एवानन्दमयो ह्यानन्दभुक्चेतोमुखः

प्राज्ञस्तृतीयः पादः ॥ ५

yatra supto na kañcana kāmaṃ kāmayate na kañcana svapnaṃ paśyati tatsuṣuptam । suṣuptasthāna ekībhūtaḥ prajñānaghana evānandamayo hyānandabhukcetomukhaḥ prājñastṛtīyaḥ pādaḥ ॥ 5

प०) यत्र सुप्तः न कञ्चन कामं कामयते न कञ्चन स्वप्नं पश्यति तत् सुषुप्तम् । सुषुप्त–स्थानः एकीभूतः प्रज्ञ–अन्–अघनः एव आनन्दमयः हि आनन्द–भुक् चेतोमुखः प्राज्ञः तृतीयः पादः ॥

अ०) यत्र [0] सुप्तः [m1/1] , when the asleep one,

कञ्चन [0] कामं [m2/1] न [0] कामयते [लट् iii/1] , any desire not wills,

कञ्चन [0] स्वप्नं [m2/1] न [0] पश्यति [लट् iii/1] ; any dream not sees,

तत् [n1/1] सुषुप्तम् [n2/1] । it deep sleep (is).

सुषुप्तस्थानः [m1/1] the one in deep sleep state एकीभूतः [m1/1] the integrated one प्रज्ञानघनः [m1/1] the solidified one एव [0] like आनन्दमयः [m1/1] blissful हि [0] Umm/Uhh आनन्दभुक् [m1/1] the experiencer of bliss चेतोमुखः [m1/1] the conscious faced प्राज्ञः [m1/1] the sentient तृतीयः [m1/1] third पादः [m1/1] phase ॥

5 Deep sleep is the third pillar. For sure senses are turned off. Intellect is off as well. Memory? Certainly no memories in the way.

O such a delight it is to go to this state. So many yearn for sound sleep. How refreshing it is!

The body really needs it. Limbs get their restoration. The mind springs back to form after such deep rest.

Does anyone deny this state? Restarting, booting up mate. Even smart phones need it all the time.

Desires are thrown aside. Aversion and bitterness is forgotten.

Much sought for state. Many miracles and discoveries a deep sleep can anchor. Bleeding hearts can be stemmed, broken marriages repaired and so much love, forgiveness and awareness can result.

A deep Meditation is likened to deep rest. Since it restores innocence, confidence and clarity of vision.

Sahaj Samadhi Meditation is a natural and profound technique to achieve deep rest.

Restful. Blissful. Essential. Pragya is thy name.

*Notice such a beautiful rendering of the three states or phases of living matter.*

- *In the **wakeful** state, the being has been termed as the **Emperor**. In the sense of most resourceful, intelligent and powerful. Isn't this the way most of us go about?*
- *In the **dream** state, the being has been termed as the **one with a Spark**. In the sense that when one is dreaming, one usually appears inert and so this clarifies.*
- *In the **deep sleep** state, the being has been termed as the **Blissful one**. We have all noticed that anyone enjoying deep rest and contentment looks so divine and happy.*

# Magic of 19

Various scriptures describe the human mind body complex using different numbers. The Bhagavad Gita uses the numbers 8 and 10 in different verses. The Vijnana Bhairava by Swami Lakshman Joo in its commentary of the $54^{th}$ verse points to 36 elements in creation. Guruji also said this during Maha Shivaratri 2016 at Bangalore Ashram.

Out of these, one-less-than-twenty i.e. 19 facets can be culled on the physical plane: Bones-Muscles-Nerves-Organs-Fluids, five breaths, five senses, mind-intellect-ego-citta-SELF = 20 Minus ONE the SELF = 19.

A Centered Triangular Number given by $(3n^2+3n+2)/2$ results in 19 for n=3.

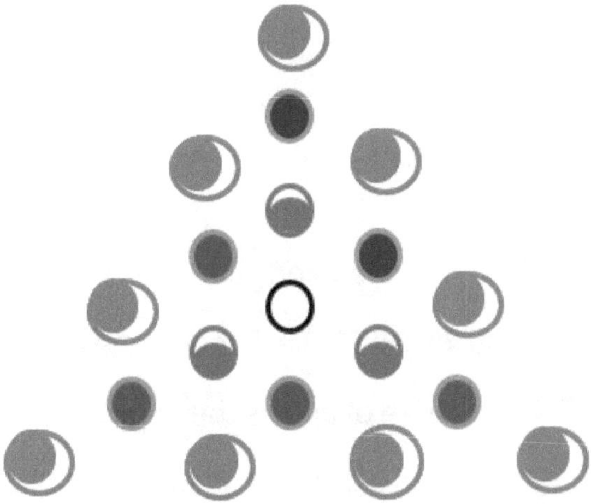

# Verse 6 Ceaseless Change

एष सर्वेश्वर एष सर्वज्ञ एषोऽन्तर्याम्येष योनिः सर्वस्य प्रभवाप्ययौ हि भूतानाम् ॥ ६

eṣa sarveśvara eṣa sarvajña eṣo'ntaryāmyeṣa yoniḥ sarvasya prabhavāpyayau hi bhūtānām ॥ 6

प०) एषः सर्वेश्वरः एषः सर्वज्ञः एषः अन्तर्यामी एषः योनिः सर्वस्य प्रभव–अप्ययौ हि भूतानाम् ॥

अ०) एषः $^{m1/1}$ सर्वेश्वरः $^{m1/1}$ , एषः $^{m1/1}$ सर्वज्ञः $^{m1/1}$ , एषः $^{m1/1}$ अन्तर्यामी $^{m1/1}$ , सर्वस्य $^{m6/1}$ एषः $^{m1/1}$ योनिः $^{m1/1}$, भूतानाम् $^{m6/3}$ हि $^{0}$ प्रभवाप्ययौ $^{m2/2}$ ॥

अन्तर्यामी from stem अन्तर्यामिन् $^{m}$ ।

एषः सर्वेश्वरः = it is the Lord of all and sundry. एषः सर्वज्ञः = it is the all-knowing. एषः अन्तर्यामी = it is the one deeply ingrained. सर्वस्य एषः योनिः = of all it is the womb.

भूतानाम् हि प्रभवाप्ययौ = of all sentient and non-sentient beings, moreover, it is the cause of birth and death / ceaseless change.

6 Who experiences these states? The soul within. The space within.

The divinity and the beauty that we all are made up of experiences Waking, Dreaming, Deep Sleep. That something which is alive inside.

Life is the experiment and the experience. The Actor is the act, the imagination and the stillness all rolled into one.

Do only humans go through the triad? Have you considered the flora and fauna? For sure all living beings go to sleep and wake up and move about. Perhaps some animals like the pet Alsatians also dream. May not be stretching it if one thought that Roses in the garden were scheming or that yonder Cloud was dreaming!

# Verse 7 OM Brahman Neti Neti

नान्तःप्रज्ञं न बहिष्प्रज्ञं नोभयतःप्रज्ञं न प्रज्ञानघनं न प्रज्ञं नाप्रज्ञम् ।

अदृष्टमव्यवहार्यमग्राह्यमलक्षणमचिन्त्यमव्यपदेश्यमेकात्मप्रत्ययसारं

प्रपञ्चोपशमं शान्तं शिवमद्वैतं चतुर्थं मन्यन्ते स आत्मा स विज्ञेयः ॥ ७

nāntaḥprajñaṃ na bahiṣprajñaṃ nobhayataḥprajñaṃ na prajñānaghanaṃ na prajñaṃ nāprajñam ।
adṛṣṭamavyavahāryamagrāhyamalakṣaṇamacintyamavyapadeśyamekātmapratyayasāraṃ prapañcopaśamaṃ śāntaṃ śivamadvaitaṃ caturthaṃ manyante sa ātmā sa vijñeyaḥ ॥ 7

प०) न अन्तःप्रज्ञं न बहिष्–प्रज्ञं न उभयतःप्रज्ञं न प्रज्ञानघनं न प्रज्ञं न अप्रज्ञम् । अदृष्टम् अव्यवहार्यम् अग्राह्यम् अलक्षणम् अचिन्त्यम् अव्यपदेश्यम् एक–आत्म–प्रत्यय–सारं प्रपञ्च–उपशमं शान्तं शिवम् अद्वैतं चतुर्थं मन्यन्ते सः आत्मा सः विज्ञेयः ॥

अ०) (ते) चतुर्थं [n2/1] मन्यन्ते [लट् iii/3] ,

They the wise regarding the 4th state opine,

न [0] अन्तःप्रज्ञं [n2/1] , न बहिष्प्रज्ञं [n2/1] , न उभयतःप्रज्ञं [n2/1] , न प्रज्ञानघनं [n2/1] , न प्रज्ञं [n2/1] , न अप्रज्ञम् [n2/1] ।

(It is) not only sentient in the inside, not only sentient in the outside, cannot be said to be only sentient both inside and outside, not solidified, not consciousness, not unconsciousness.

अदृष्टम् n2/1 अव्यवहार्यम् n2/1 अग्राह्यम् n2/1 अलक्षणम् n2/1

अचिन्त्यम् n2/1 अव्यपदेश्यम् n2/1 । (It is) not visible, not transactional, not graspable, not definable, not ponderable, not describable.

एकात्मप्रत्ययसारं n2/1 प्रपञ्चोपशमं n2/1 शान्तं n2/1 शिवम् n2/1

अद्वैतं n2/1 । (It is) the essence of the experiences of the soul, the confluence of the great elements, peacefulness, auspiciousness, non-dual / not separable into parts.

सः m1/1 आत्मा m1/1 , that is the Soul

सः m1/1 विज्ञेयः तव्य PoPP m1/1 ॥ that is to be understood.

7 Have you considered the foundations? The state that the other states rest upon? The state that cannot fit into the triad because it is too BIG.

Simply see your breath. Goes in. Comes out. And doesn't move at times. What about the switch from in to out? Or out to still?

Easily you are the Father and the Flame and the Son. But these three states are too well defined and sometimes you are the Stranger as well. When no one can define you.

Think about it. Ponder on that which is neither Time and neither Space and neither both. Contemplate on that which gave birth to time and space and remains untouched by both.

Is there something that is not matter and not anti-matter? For sure there is something that is beyond energy and matter. Beyond mind and emotion. Beyond the living and the non-living.

See the movie and become aware of the white screen. See the rope and wonder why it suddenly appeared to move. Is air alone the cause? Or did the gloomy weather and doubting mind conjure it up?

For sure there is more to than what meets the eye. There are lands and oceans where man has never ventured forth and not probed. There are galaxies where Newton's laws laugh and sing and keep changing. Where the math is so different a human intellect cannot divine.

This is the verse that is eulogized in Vedantic lore as

नेति नेति । न इति न इति । **Not this. Not this...**

And it is so true. As one grows up, one drops old concepts. The best toys no longer interest. And slowly steadily when tries to express or explain the TRUTH, no words come. No words are adequate. No statements or explanations can deliver.

# 3 ॐ त्रीणि

The number three looks very similar to the symbol OM, signifying its inherent triple quality. In Sanskrit, the number three or त्रीणि is always in plural.

# Verse 8 AUM = Waking Dreaming Sleeping

सोऽयमात्माऽध्यक्षरमोङ्कारोऽधिमात्रं पादा मात्रा मात्राश्च पादा अकार उकारो मकार इति ॥ ८

so'yamātmā'dhyakṣaramoṅkāro'dhimātraṃ pādā mātrā mātrāśca pādā akāra ukāro makāra iti ॥ 8

प०) सः अयम् आत्मा अध्यक्षरम् ओङ्कारः अधिमात्रं पादाः मात्राः मात्राः च पादाः अकारः उकारः मकारः इति ॥

अ०)

सः [m1/1] अध्यक्षरम् [n1/1] ओङ्कारः [m1/1] अयम् [n1/1] आत्मा [m1/1],

पादाः [m1/3] मात्राः [f1/3] अधिमात्रं [n2/1],

मात्राः [f1/3] च [0] पादाः [m1/3],

अकारः [m1/1] उकारः [m1/1] मकारः [m1/1] इति [0] ॥

सः अध्यक्षरम् ओङ्कारः अयम् आत्मा that imperishable Word Om this Soul (is). पादाः मात्राः अधिमात्रं the phases correspond to each letter. मात्राः च पादाः And the letters correspond to each phase.

अकारः उकारः मकारः इति **A**sound **U**sound **M**sound thus.

8 So what to do? Does it mean I shall never attain Brahman? I shall never drop my past or my sorrow?

No No. Learn the proper way to chant. Learn the mahavakyas and the mahamantras from the Master.

The Guru teaches that the sacred syllable AUM must always be used as a prefix to other auspicious sounds.

e.g.
Om Namah Shivaya.
Om Namo Bhagavate Vasudevaya.
Om Hare Rama Hare Rama, Rama Rama Hare Hare, Hare Krishna Hare Krishna, Krishna Krishna Hare Hare.
Om Namo Narayanaya…

And then the magic unfolds. The letters of the sacred syllable infuse and impregnate one's consciousness with the trinity that is LOVE JOY ENTHUSIASM. One's prana begins to flow correctly and one's chakras open up one by one.

# Verse 9 A-Wake = the Emperorship

जागरितस्थानो वैश्वानरोऽकारः प्रथमा मात्राऽऽप्तेरादिमत्वाद्वाऽऽप्नोति ह

वै सर्वान्कामानादिश्च भवति य एवं वेद ॥ ९

jāgaritasthāno vaiśvānaro'kāraḥ prathamā mātrā''pterādimattvādvā''pnoti ha vai

sarvānkāmānādiśca bhavati ya evaṃ veda ॥ 9

प०) जागरित–स्थानः वैश्वानरः अकारः प्रथमा मात्रा आप्तेः आदिमत्वात् वा आप्नोति ह वै सर्वान् कामान् आदिः च भवति यः एवं वेद ॥

अ०) जागरितस्थानः [m1/1] वैश्वानरः [m1/1] अकारः [m1/1] प्रथमा [f1/1] मात्रा [f1/1] , आप्तेः [f6/1] आदिमत्वात् [m5/1] वा [0] ।

यः [m1/1] एवं [0] वेद [लट् iii/1], सर्वान् [m2/3] कामान् [m2/3] आप्नोति [लट् iii/1], ह [0] वै [0] आदिः [m1/3] च [0] भवति [लट् iii/1] ॥

By 3.4.83 विदो लिटो वा । वेद , वेत्ति are both forms for लट् iii/1.

जागरितस्थानः वैश्वानरः अकारः प्रथमा मात्रा the wakeful state termed as Vaishvanara = Emperor corresponds to **A**sound the first letter. आप्तेः आदिमत्वात् वा (who is) of universal presence and from the beginning.

यः एवं वेद The one who so understands.

सर्वान् कामान् आप्नोति all objectives attains. ह वै आदिः च भवति Indeed and the foremost he becomes.

9 When one chants AUM properly as taught by the Master, the **A**sound vibrates at the lower chakras, especially the mooladhara and the swadishthana.

This ensures optimal functioning of the senses and the intellect, thus one is able to perform well at work and at home.

Bit by bit one climbs the ladder and achieves success and fame. One delivers ever increasing targets and is able to touch international heights.

# Verse 10 U-Dream = the Spark of Infinity

स्वप्नस्थानस्तैजस उकारो द्वितीया मात्रोत्कर्षादुभयत्वाद्वोत्कर्षति ह वै ज्ञानसन्ततिं समानश्च भवति नास्याब्रह्मवित्कुले भवति य एवं वेद ॥ १०

svapnasthānastaijasa ukāro dvitīyā mātrotkarṣādubhayatvādvotkarṣati ha vai jñānasantatiṃ samānaśca bhavati nāsyābrahmavitkule bhavati ya evaṃ veda ǁ 10

प०) स्वप्न–स्थानः तैजसः उकारः द्वितीया मात्रा उत्कर्षात् उभयत्वात् वा उत्कर्षति ह वै ज्ञान–सन्ततिं समानः च भवति न अस्य अब्रह्मवित् कुले भवति यः एवं वेद ॥

अ०) स्वप्नस्थानः [m1/1] तैजसः [m1/1] उकारः [m1/1] द्वितीया [f1/1] मात्रा [f1/1], उत्कर्षात् [m5/1] उभयत्वात् [m5/1] वा [0] । यः [m1/1] एवं [0] वेद [लट् iii/1], ज्ञानसन्ततिं [m2/1] उत्कर्षति [लट् iii/1], समानः [m1/1] च [0] भवति [लट् iii/1]। ह वै कुले [m7/1] अस्य [m6/1] अब्रह्मवित् [n2/1] न [0] भवति [लट् iii/1] ॥ स्वप्नस्थानः तैजसः उकारः द्वितीया मात्रा Dream state calledTaijasa = the one with Spark corresponds to **U**sound the second letter. उत्कर्षात् उभयत्वात् वा (which is) from improvement and double-edged gain. यः एवं वेद The one who so understands. ज्ञानसन्ततिं उत्कर्षति he broadens the traditional knowledge base. समानः च भवति And is a secular visionary. ह वै कुले अस्य अब्रह्मवित् न भवति Indeed among his descendants none is born ignorant.

**10** At the heart center one experiences a fluid state that is not limited by the body or the mind. This state is the source of emotions and in this state one can go anywhere and experience anything.

No resource crunch, no relationship bitterness comes in the way. All goals seem puny, the one whom one wants comes straight to one's arms.

To the one who can dream, to him the pathways to greatness beckon.

When one chants AUM properly as taught by the Master, the **U**sound vibrates at the heart center. This frees up all knots and restores love, faith and innocence.

# Verse 11 M-Sleep O I'm so Happy

सुषुप्तस्थानः प्राज्ञो मकारस्तृतीया मात्रा मितेरपीतेर्वा मिनोति ह वा इदं सर्वमपीतिश्च भवति य एवं वेद ॥ ११

suṣuptasthānaḥ prājño makārastṛtīyā mātrā miterapītervā minoti ha vā idaṃ sarvamapītiśca bhavati ya evaṃ veda ‖ 11

प०) सुषुप्त–स्थानः प्राज्ञः मकारः तृतीया मात्रा मितेः अपीतेः वा मिनोति ह वै इदं सर्वम् अपीतिः च भवति यः एवं वेद ॥

अ०) सुषुप्तस्थानः [m1/1] प्राज्ञः [m1/1] मकारः [m1/1] तृतीया [f1/1] मात्रा [f1/1], मितेः [m5/1] अपीतेः [m6/1] वा ।

यः [m1/1] एवं [0] वेद [लट् iii/1], (सः) इदं [n2/1] सर्वम् [n2/1] मिनोति [लट् iii/1]।

ह वै अपीतिः [m1/1] च भवति [लट् iii/1]॥

वै + इदं=>sandhi=>वा इदं ।

मकारः तृतीया मात्रा **M**sound the third letter of AUM.

मितेः अपीतेः वा from discernment of the ultimate.

यः एवं वेद The one who so understands, He this all discerns. ह वै अपीतिः च भवति Indeed and becomes immortal.

11 When one's awareness rise to the higher chakras, at the third eye, then one is able to sift and discriminate. There is also the state of bliss at the sahasrara chakra, where one experiences deep rest.

One can then sense all the changing and also become aware of something that remains unchanged throughout.

This is the key to immortality.

When one chants AUM properly as taught by the Master, the **M**sound vibrates between the eyebrows and goes higher up as well. This frees up the *chitta* so that one can experience bliss, defenselessness, and eternity.

# Verse 12 TURIYA TRANSCENDENTAL

अमात्रश्चतुर्थोऽव्यवहार्यः प्रपञ्चोपशमः शिवोऽद्वैत एवमोङ्कार आत्मैव संविशत्यात्मनाऽऽत्मानं य एवं वेद य एवं वेद ॥ १२ ॥

amātraścaturtho'vyavahāryaḥ prapañcopaśamaḥ śivo'dvaita evamoṅkāra ātmaiva saṃviśatyātmanā''tmānaṃ ya evaṃ veda ya evaṃ veda ॥ 12 ॥

प०) अमात्रः चतुर्थः अव्यवहार्यः प्रपञ्च–उपशमः शिवः अद्वैतः एवम् ओङ्कारः आत्मा एव संविशति आत्मना आत्मानं यः एवं वेद् यः एवं वेद् ॥

अ०) अमात्रः [m1/1] चतुर्थः [m1/1] अव्यवहार्यः [m1/1] प्रपञ्चोपशमः [m1/1] शिवः [m1/1] अद्वैतः [m1/1] , एवम् [0] ओङ्कारः [m1/1] आत्मा [m1/1] ।
यः [m1/1] एवं [0] वेद् [लट् iii/1] , आत्मना [m3/1] आत्मानं [m2/1] एव [0] संविशति [लट् iii/1] ।
यः [m1/1] एवं [0] वेद् [लट् iii/1] ॥ *repeated for emphasis.*

यः एवं वेद् , आत्मना आत्मानं एव संविशति the one who so understands, by the Self into the Self alone he merges.

12 Having known so many things of this world, having lived a full life and having had so many challenging adventures, one finally comes to the point of relaxation. **One understands that one knows not**. There is an infinity to experience but it cannot be known or encapsulated within theories.

Having applied oneself thoroughly, having given 100% effort and shouldered all one's responsibilities, a time comes to drop it all.

Then one experiences the foundation state, the transcendental state that is ever present but hard to ascertain. This is called the TURIYA state in Vedantic lore. This is achieved only in deep meditation, in SAMADHI.

At the end, the state of deep stillness when one imbibes, one's soul merges into the cosmic soul.

This state dawns only for the wise, only for the one who has persevered patiently till the end.

---

END

## Latin Transliteration Chart

International Alphabet of Sanskrit Transliteration (I.A.S.T.)

| | | | | | | | | | |
|---|---|---|---|---|---|---|---|---|---|
| a | ā | i | ī | u | ū | ṛ | ṝ | ḷ | |
| अ | आ | इ | ई | उ | ऊ | ऋ | ॠ | ऌ | |
| | | | | | | ◌ृ | ◌ॄ | ◌ॢ | |
| e | ai | o | au | ṃ | m̐ | ḥ | Ardha Visarga | oṃ | |
| ए | ऐ | ओ | औ | ◌ं | ◌ँ | ◌ः | ᳲ | ॐ | |
| Consonants are shown with a vowel ‘a= अ’ for uttering | | | | | | | | | |
| ka | क | ca | च | ṭa | ट | ta | त | pa | प |
| kha | ख | cha | छ | ṭha | ठ | tha | थ | pha | फ |
| ga | ग | ja | ज | ḍa | ड | da | द | ba | ब |
| gha | घ | jha | झ | ḍha | ढ | dha | ध | bha | भ |
| ṅa | ङ | ña | ञ | ṇa | ण | na | न | ma | म |
| | | | | | | | | | |
| ya | ra | la | va | | ḷa | ‘ | | | |
| य | र | ल | व | | ळ | ऽ | | | |
| | | | | | **Consonant only** | | | | |
| śa | ṣa | sa | ha | | **ka** | क्अ = क | | | |
| श | ष | स | ह | | **k** | क् | | | |

## Verses for Chanting

॥ अथ माण्डूक्योपनिषद् ॥

ॐ भद्रं कर्णेभिः शृणुयाम देवाः । भद्रं पश्येमाक्षभिर्यजत्राः ।

स्थिरैरङ्गैस्तुष्टुवांसस्तनूभिः । व्यशेम देवहितं यदायुः ॥

स्वस्ति न इन्द्रो वृद्धश्रवाः । स्वस्ति नः पूषा विश्ववेदाः ।

स्वस्ति नस्तार्क्ष्यो अरिष्टनेमिः । स्वस्ति नो बृहस्पतिर्दधातु ॥

ॐ शान्तिः शान्तिः शान्तिः ॥

॥ अथ प्रथमः खण्डः ॥

ओमित्येतदक्षरमिदं सर्वं तस्योपव्याख्यानं भूतं भवद्भविष्यदिति

सर्वमोङ्कार एव । यच्चान्यत्त्रिकालातीतं तदप्योङ्कार एव ॥ १

सर्वं ह्येतद् ब्रह्मायमात्मा ब्रह्म सोऽयमात्मा चतुष्पात् ॥ २

॥ इति माण्डूक्योपनिषदि प्रथमः खण्डः ॥

॥ अथ द्वितीयः खण्डः ॥

जागरितस्थानो बहिष्प्रज्ञः सप्ताङ्ग एकोनविंशतिमुखः स्थूलभुग्वैश्वानरः

प्रथमः पादः ॥ ३

स्वप्नस्थानोऽन्तःप्रज्ञः सप्ताङ्ग एकोनविंशतिमुखः प्रविविक्तभुक्तैजसो द्वितीयः पादः ॥ ४

यत्र सुप्तो न कञ्चन कामं कामयते न कञ्चन स्वप्नं पश्यति तत्सुषुप्तम् । सुषुप्तस्थान एकीभूतः प्रज्ञानघन एवानन्दमयो ह्यानन्दभुक्चेतोमुखः प्राज्ञस्तृतीयः पादः ॥ ५

एष सर्वेश्वर एष सर्वज्ञ एषोऽन्तर्याम्येष योनिः सर्वस्य प्रभवाप्ययौ हि भूतानाम् ॥ ६

नान्तःप्रज्ञं न बहिष्प्रज्ञं नोभयतःप्रज्ञं न प्रज्ञानघनं न प्रज्ञं नाप्रज्ञम् । अदृष्टमव्यवहार्यमग्राह्यमलक्षणमचिन्त्यमव्यपदेश्यमेकात्मप्रत्ययसारं प्रपञ्चोपशमं शान्तं शिवमद्वैतं चतुर्थं मन्यन्ते स आत्मा स विज्ञेयः ॥ ७

## ॥ इति माण्डूक्योपनिषदि द्वितीयः खण्डः ॥

## ॥ अथ तृतीयः खण्डः ॥

सोऽयमात्माऽध्यक्षरमोङ्कारोऽधिमात्रं पादा मात्रा मात्राश्च पादा अकार उकारो मकार इति ॥ ८

जागरितस्थानो वैश्वानरोऽकारः प्रथमा मात्राऽऽप्तेरादिमत्वाद्वाऽऽप्नोति ह वै सर्वान्कामानादिश्च भवति य एवं वेद ॥ ९

स्वप्नस्थानस्तैजस उकारो द्वितीया मात्रोत्कर्षादुभयत्वाद्वोत्कर्षति ह वै ज्ञानसन्ततिं समानश्च भवति नास्याब्रह्मवित्कुले भवति य एवं वेद ॥ १०

सुषुप्तस्थानः प्राज्ञो मकारस्तृतीया मात्रा मितेरपीतेर्वा मिनोति ह वा इदꣳ सर्वमपीतिश्च भवति य एवं वेद ॥ ११

॥ इति माण्डूक्योपनिषदि तृतीयः खण्डः ॥

॥ अथ चतुर्थः खण्डः ॥

अमात्रश्चतुर्थोऽव्यवहार्यः प्रपञ्चोपशमः शिवोऽद्वैत एवमोङ्कार आत्मैव संविशत्यात्मनाऽऽत्मानं य एवं वेद य एवं वेद ॥ १२ ॥

॥ इति ॥

ॐ

भ॒द्रं कर्णे॑भिः शृणु॒याम॑ देवाः । भ॒द्रं प॑श्येमा॒क्षभि॒र्यज॑त्राः ।
स्थि॒रैरङ्गै॑स्तुष्टु॒वाꣳस॑स्त॒नूभिः॑ । व्यशे॑म दे॒वहि॑तं॒ यदायुः॑ ॥
स्व॒स्ति न॒ इन्द्रो॑ वृ॒द्धश्र॑वाः । स्व॒स्ति नः॑ पू॒षा वि॒श्ववे॑दाः ।
स्व॒स्ति न॒स्तार्क्ष्यो॒ अरि॑ष्टनेमिः । स्व॒स्ति नो॒ बृह॒स्पति॑र्दधातु ॥
ॐ शान्तिः॒ शान्तिः॒ शान्तिः॑ ॥

# Sanskrit Grammar

Sandhis separated word by word पदच्छेद (प०),

Verses in prose order अन्वय (अ०), and with विभक्ति Cases have been listed.

<u>Abbreviations</u>

Nouns

**m** masculine, **f** feminine, **n** neuter; **V** vocative
**1/1** = vibhakti case from 1 to 7/number 1 to 3

Indeclinables (uninflected nouns or verbs) **0**
In Sanskrit the **adverbs** are mostly uninflected.

Verbs

**iii/1** = person i to iii / number 1 to 3

**PPP** = Past Participle Passive = क्त

**PPA** = Past Participle Active = क्तवत्

**PrPA** = Present Participle Active = शतृ / शानच्

**FPA** = Future Participle Active = लृट् + शतृ

**PoPP** = Potential Participle Passive = य, तव्य, अनीयर् (gerundive)

Anusvara and Makara have been kept as they are in the Padacheda, without changing each Anusvara, to avoid overwork typos. E.g. ideally इदं should be written as इदम् but it has been left unchanged in Padacheda.

Since Sanskrit is an inflectional language, the **spelling of the same word** changes as per context or usage. Hence words can be **placed anywhere** in a sentence, as in poetic use, without change in meaning. The matrix shows how.

**Verb inflections in Sanskrit - a sample chart**

| 982 गमॢ गतौ – to go, also in the sense of attainment | | | |
|---|---|---|---|
| Present Tense Active voice लट् कर्त्तरि | | | |
| Person/no | singular | dual | plural |
| Third | गच्छति [iii/1] | गच्छतः [iii/2] | गच्छन्ति [iii/3] |
| Second | गच्छसि [ii/1] | गच्छथः [ii/2] | गच्छथ [ii/3] |
| First | गच्छामि [i/1] | गच्छावः [i/2] | गच्छामः [i/3] |

**Noun declensions in Sanskrit - a sample chart**

| Masculine stem, vowel अ ending | | | |
|---|---|---|---|
| (र्–आ–म्–अ) राम [m] Lord's name | | | |
| | singular [1] | dual [2] | plural [3] |
| 1 Doer | रामः [1/1] | रामौ [1/2] | रामाः [1/3] |
| 2 Object | रामम् [2/1] | रामौ [2/2] | रामान् [2/3] |
| 3 by | रामेण [3/1] | रामाभ्याम् [3/2] | रामैः [3/3] |
| 4 for | रामाय [4/1] | रामाभ्याम् [4/2] | रामेभ्यः [4/3] |
| 5 from | रामात् [5/1] | रामाभ्याम् [5/2] | रामेभ्यः [5/3] |
| 6 of | रामस्य [6/1] | रामयोः [6/2] | रामाणाम् [6/3] |
| 7 in | रामे [7/1] | रामयोः [7/2] | रामेषु [7/3] |
| Vocative | हे राम [V/1] | हे रामौ [V/2] | हे रामाः [V/3] |

| Masculine stem, consonant त् ending | | | |
|---|---|---|---|
| मरुत् m Wind, Breeze, Air | | | |
| | singular [1] | dual [2] | plural [3] |
| 1 Doer | मरुत् 1/1 | मरुतौ 1/2 | मरुतः 1/3 |
| 2 Object | मरुतम् 2/1 | मरुतौ 2/2 | मरुतः 2/3 |
| 3 by | मरुता 3/1 | मरुद्भ्याम् 3/2 | मरुद्भिः 3/3 |
| 4 for | मरुते 4/1 | मरुद्भ्याम् 4/2 | मरुद्भ्यः 4/3 |
| 5 from | मरुतः 5/1 | मरुद्भ्याम् 5/2 | मरुद्भ्यः 5/3 |
| 6 of | मरुतः 6/1 | मरुतोः 6/2 | मरुताम् 6/3 |
| 7 in | मरुति 7/1 | मरुतोः 7/2 | मरुत्सु 7/3 |
| Vocative | हे मरुत् V/1 | हे मरुतौ V/2 | हे मरुतः V/3 |

Moods and Tenses in Sanskrit

| | | |
|---|---|---|
| 1 | लट् | Present Tense |
| 2 | लुङ् | Aorist Past Tense,*before from now onwards* |
| 3 | लङ् | Imperfect Past Tense – *before from yesterday onwards* |
| 4 | लिट् | Perfect Past Tense – *distant unseen past* |
| 5 | लृट् | Simple Future Tense – *now onwards* |
| 6 | लुट् | Periphrastic Future Tense – *tomorrow onwards* |
| 7 | लृङ् | Conditional Mood - *if/then in past or future* |
| 8 | लोट् | Imperative Mood – *request* |
| 9 | विधि–लिङ् | Potential Mood – *order विधिलिङ्* (also known as Optative Mood) |
| 10 | आशीर्–लिङ् | Benedictive Mood – *blessing आशीर्लिङ्* (also used in the sense of a curse) |

## Conjugation process of Verb

मन्यन्ते = they opine, they think. Verse 7

Root 1176 √ मनँ ज्ञाने । to think, meditate

1.3.1 भूवादयो धातवः। मनँ = मन्अँ

1.3.2 उपदेशेऽजनुनासिक इत् । 1.3.9 तस्य लोपः। मन्

3.4.69 लः कर्मणि च भावे चाकर्मकेभ्यः। मन्

3.2.123 वर्तमाने लट् । 3.4.77 लस्य । मन् + लँट्

1.3.3 हलन्त्यम् । 1.3.9 तस्य लोपः । मन् + लँ

1.3.2 उपदेशेऽजनुनासिक इत् । 1.3.9 तस्य लोपः । मन् + ल्

3.4.78 तिप्तस्झिसिप्थस्थमिब्वस्मस् तातांझथासाथांध्वमिड्वहिमहिङ् ।

1.4.100 तङानावात्मनेपदम् ।

मन् + तातांझ । we are conjugating third person

1.4.101 तिङस्त्रीणि त्रीणि प्रथममध्यमोत्तमाः ।

1.4.102 तान्येकवचनद्विवचनबहुवचनान्येकशः ।

मन् + झ । plural

1.4.108 शेषे प्रथमः । मन् + झ । this is called "प्रथमः" i.e. the **first and most** used in language i.e. third person.

3.4.113 तिङ्शित्सार्वधातुकम् । मन् + झ

3.1.69 दिवादिभ्यः श्यन् । मन् + श्यन् + झ

3.4.113 तिङ्शित्सार्वधातुकम् । मन् + श्यन् + झ

1.3.3 हलन्त्यम् । 1.3.8 लशक्वतद्धिते । 1.3.9 तस्य लोपः ।

मन् + य + झ । 7.1.3 झोऽन्तः । मन् + य + अन्त ।

3.4.79 टित आत्मनेपदानां टेरे । मन् + य + अन्ते ।

1.2.4 सार्वधातुकमपित् । 1.1.5 ग्क्ङिति च । श्यन् affix does not undergo guna. मन् + य + अन्ते ।

6.1.97 अतो गुणे । मन् + य् + अन्ते । sandhi drops अकारः।

8.3.24 नश्चापदान्तस्य झलि । मन् + य् + अंते । Anusvara.

8.4.58 अनुस्वारस्य ययि परसवर्णः । मन् + य् + अन्ते ।

Anusvara again changes to नकारः ।

मन् + य् + अन्ते = मन्यन्ते लट् iii/3 ।

## Declension process of Noun

ओङ्कारः = The Sacred Syllable. Verse 1 and 12.

Stem Oñkar ओङ्कार m => ओङ्कारः m1/1

ओङ्कारः = ॐकारः = the sound represented by the symbol ॐ ।

1.2.45 अर्थवदधातुरप्रत्ययः प्रातिपदिकम् । ओङ्कार

1.2.46 कृत्तद्धितसमासाश्च । 3.1.1 प्रत्ययः । 3.1.2 परश्च ।

4.1.1 ङ्याप्प्रातिपदिकात्

4.1.2 स्वौजस-

मौट्छष्टाभ्याम्भिस्ङेभ्याम्भ्यस्ङसिभ्याम्भ्यस्ङसोसाम्ङ्योस्सुप् ।

1.4.104 विभक्तिश्च । 1.4.103 सुपः = use one of these vibhakti suffix. ओङ्कार + सुँ ।

1.4.22 द्व्येकयोर्द्विवचनैकवचने = singular number taken.

ओङ्कार + सुँ ।

1.1.43 सुड्–अनपुंसकस्य । ओङ्कार + सउँ ।

1.3.2 उपदेशेऽजनुनासिक इत् । 1.3.9 तस्य लोपः। ओङ्कार +स् ।

1.3.4 न विभक्तौ तुस्माः = final सकारः of a Vibhakti is not a tag letter. ओङ्कार + स् ।

8.2.66 ससजुषो रुः । ओङ्कार + रुँ । ओङ्कार + र् उँ ।

1.3.2 उपदेशेऽजनुनासिक इत् । 1.3.9 तस्य लोपः। ओङ्कार + र् ।

8.3.15 खर्–अवसानयोः विसर्जनीयः। Repha to Visarga when facing a full stop.

ओङ्कार + ःः = ओङ्कारः m1/1 ।

*Masculine. First case singular*. Om. The Highest. The Supreme. Shiva. Purusha. Tao.

# References

https://www.ashtangayoga.info/philosophy/sanskrit-and-devanagari/transliteration-tool/

http://spokensanskrit.org/
http://bhagavadgita.org.in/sanskrit
https://upanishads.org.in/upanishads
https://www.sanskritworld.in/index/Sanskrittool

Uma Mohan sings the Upanishad verses
https://www.youtube.com/watch?v=Bi3VBOqA8i8

Stephanie Simoes
https://www.academia.edu/27386976/Mandukya_Upanishad_Word-for-Word_Translation_with_Transliteration_and_Grammatical_Notes

KLV Sastry & Anantarama Sastri – Sabda Manjari 1961– Reprint - 2013 – RS Vadhyar & Sons, Palghat.

Shripad Damodar Satwalekar – माण्डूक्य उपनिषद् - 1st –1952 – Swadhyay Mandal Anand Ashram, Killa Pardi, Surat.

Swami Rama – Mandukya Upanishad, Enlightenment without God - 1st – 1982 – The Himalayan International Institute, Honesdale USA.

Swami Devarupananda – मन्त्रपुष्पम् - 4th – 2010 – Ramakrishna Math, Khar, Mumbai.

Ashwini Kumar Aggarwal – Dhatupatha of Panini – 2nd – 2017 – Devotees of Sri Sri Ravi Shankar Ashram, Punjab.

# Epilogue

When one stops still and listens, a sound is heard.
Felt within.

Perhaps it is that Om, the un-struck without origin.

सर्वे भवन्तु सुखिनः । सर्वे सन्तु निरामयाः ।

सर्वे भद्राणि पश्यन्तु । मा कश्चिद् दुःख भाग् भवेत् ॥

ॐ शान्तिः शान्तिः शान्तिः ॥

When faith has blossomed in life,
Every step is led by the Divine.

Sri Sri Ravi Shankar

**Om Namah Shivaya**

जय गुरुदेव

www.ingramcontent.com/pod-product-compliance
Lightning Source LLC
Chambersburg PA
CBHW051402280526
45784CB00007B/3069
* 9 7 8 1 0 9 9 1 9 3 5 4 5 *